{Vintage Collage Journals}

GENTILE DA FABRIANO

L.30
SAN MARINO
COURVOISIER S.A.

NUOVA TO

ITALY

LA FENICE

VENEZIA

SEPTENTRIO

MA

VINTAGE

Collage Journals
JOURNALING WITH ANTIQUE EPHEMERA

BEVERLY MASSACHUSETTS

QUARRY BOOKS

MARYJO KOCH

Produced & Designed by Jennifer Barry

Photographs by Wendy Candelaria

Text by Carolyn Miller

First published in the United States of America by
Quarry Books, a member of
Quayside Publishing Group
100 Cummings Center, Suite 406-L
Beverly, Massachusetts 01915
Telephone: (978) 282-9590
Fax: (978) 283-2742
www.quarrybooks.com
Visit www.craftside.typepad.com for a behind-the-scenes peek at our crafty world.

Library of Congress Cataloging-in-Publication Data
Koch, Maryjo.
  Vintage collage journals : journaling with antique ephemera / Maryjo Koch.
       p. cm.
  Includes bibliographical references and index.
  ISBN-13: 978-1-59253-576-7
  ISBN-10: 1-59253-576-3
  1. Collage. 2. Diaries--Authorship. I. Title.
  TT910.K634 2009
  745.593--dc22
                              2009018471

ISBN-13: 978-1-59253-576-7
ISBN-10: 1-59253-576-3

10 9 8 7 6 5 4 3 2 1

Produced and designed by Jennifer Barry Design, Fairfax, CA
Layout Production by Kristen Hall
Photographs by Wendy Candelaria
Text by Carolyn Miller

Printed in Singapore

My
Flower
Garden
of
Treasured

Quotes
and

Poetry

POSTE ITALIANE 60 Cent.

MILANO CENTRO

ISOLA BELLA — ITALIA L.150

Arrivangen Milano
May 19

Stati Uniti D'America

114

23.12.1924

{ *Contents* }

❧

{ *Introduction* }

*E*very journal is a record of a journey, either through time or into the heart of its subject. Vintage Collage Journals *is a guide to making illustrated journals using the antique and vintage ephemera—scraps of cloth, pages from books, ribbons and trimmings—found in antique stores, secondhand shops, flea markets, and our own homes. By combining these bits of the past with various painting techniques, you can record travels real and imagined, immortalize your dinner parties, mark the cycle of the seasons in the natural world and your garden, and treasure your family's precious memories.*

Both journal *and* journey *have the same root,* jour, *French for "day," reflecting the original definition of a journal as a daily log of financial transactions, then its later meaning: a private record of an individual's daily life. The word* journey *has its origin in a time when a journey simply meant one day's travel.*

A wide variety of journals can be used for collage, from blank albums and artist's sketchbooks to vintage books such as old accounting ledgers and logbooks.

Journals ground us in a specific time and place, but they can also allow us to travel through time and space on the wings of imagination. Because they are the reflection of a unique individual perspective, journals naturally have a kind of spontaneity that printed books, which are the result of structured planning, often lack. Most journals also have an authenticity that is not often found in fiction; they are the real voice of the writer speaking to us.

Journals capture not just a day but the moments of that day that are meaningful and memorable to the writer. The writer of a journal lives twice: in the real time of the day and in the remembering of the day. Adding visual elements to a journal illuminates the words and adds an entire new level of expression to each page.

scraps of printed ephemera and memorabilia with rubber stamps, postage stamps, and other keepsakes with watercolor or gouache sketches, then recording events and memories in handwritten text, creates a rich layering of color, image, and words. The handwritten words inspire the art that embellishes the pages, and the art in turn inspires the words.

In the pages of these handmade books, we can memorialize those things that have meaning for us, from the specific details of the place where we live to the day-by-day experiences of a journey to another country.

But not all illustrated journals are grounded in reality: they can also let us travel on the wings of imagination to places we have

In the pages of handmade journals, we can memorialize those things that have meaning for us.

The history of illustrated journals began the first time an unknown man or woman added a simple sketch to the pages of a handwritten book. Illustrated travel journals have a long history of their own, beginning with the first scientific expeditions from England and Europe to other countries. Travel journals came into their own among nonscientists with the advent of "the grand tour" in the mid-seventeenth century, when wealthy young Englishmen began traveling to Europe to educate themselves in art and culture. Nature journals are another beloved category of the illustrated journal, chronicling the passage of time in an individual garden or particular rustic area. And family journals, when illustrated by collage and painting, become not just family records but valued works of art.

Anyone can create an illustrated journal using the tools and techniques in *Vintage Collage Journals*. A collage journal is one of the simplest ways to express the artistry found in each of us. Combining

never been or that do not exist, and we can even live in someone else's past or present. The possibilities of words and art are unlimited.

Using collage to adorn journal pages with antique and vintage ephemera creates layers and patterns of beautiful scraps of the past, such as old photographs and menus, sheet music, greeting cards and postcards, old letters and pieces of fabric, pressed flowers and natural objects, like feathers and leaves. These can be objects that you have collected and saved over time, or you can search for appropriate materials in shops to illustrate your particular journal. *Vintage Collage Journals* also shows you how to use such simple art techniques as scumbling and image transfer to add color and depth to your collages. The art tools and materials can be found in any art store, and none are expensive. The journals themselves can be purchased in art or stationery stores; you can even make your own journals using simple binding techniques. And you can follow the

instructions for each of the varied kinds of journals in this book exactly, or combine ideas and techniques from different projects to create your own unique books.

From travel journals to logbooks of favorite wines or collections of recipes, from an account of how your garden grew through the year to a record of your family's important milestones, lovely pieces of the past can make memories come to life again on the page for yourself and others.

{ *Tools & Materials* }

*M*ost of the tools and materials used to make the collage journals in this book are available in any good art store, including various kinds of paints, pens, brushes, and papers. The journals themselves include spiral and bound ones with handmade paper, photo albums, and vintage logbooks. Ephemera from your own boxes and shelves at home or purchased from secondhand stores, antique stores, and flea markets will make your collage journals unique to your life and your stories. Following is a list of all the tools and materials needed to make the journals in this book.

The tools of a collage artist, from paints and adhesives to a choice of brushes, pens, and cutting implements. Tool kits, carrying cases, or old cosmetic suitcases such as these shown here make convenient storage cases for a variety of tools and materials.

{ *Tools* }

PAINTS & VARNISHES

Watercolors

Gouache paints, including
  Holbein Brilliant Gold

Acrylic paints

Sennelier Walnut Stain ink

Dr. Ph. Martin's Olive
  Green ink

Oxgall

Acrylic matte varnish

Matte medium

Acrylic spray coating (fixative)

BRUSHES

Scumbling brush or No. 10 round
  brush (cut one half off to
  create a squared-off brush)

Stencil brush , ½ inch (for paste)

Old watercolor brushes, small
  and medium (for varnish
  and gouache)

Filbert brush for Holbein
  Brilliant Gold gouache

Liner brush 10/0
  (for painting narrow lines)

Good watercolor brushes

TAPES, PASTES, & GLUES

Yes! paste

Double-stick tape

Transparent tape

Blue self-release painter's tape

PENS, PENCILS, & STAMPS

Chartpak blender pens
  (P-O 201), new and old

Calligraphy pen

Micron pen, black (.005)

Colored pencils

Pencil

Eraser

Rubber stamps and ink pads

Derwent sketching pencil
  (dark wash)

CUTTING & MEASURING TOOLS

X-acto knife

Cutting mat

Japanese screw punch

Awl

Metal ruler

45-degree triangle

Scissors, pointed
  (large and small)

Bone folder

MISCELLANEOUS

Sealing wax and decorative seals

Photocopier

Flower press

Palette knife

Kraft-paper-covered brick

Heavy books

Needle and thread

{ *Materials* }

A variety of blank journals can be used for collage; spiral-bound journals and photo albums can be collaged with thicker kinds of paper, such as postcards and photographs, without making the pages bulge open. (Look for photo albums with cream-colored or white pages; if they have glassine protectors, you can simply tear them out.) Even vintage books that have already been written in, such as the logbook on pages 48–49, can be used by collaging part of the page and leaving some of the writing visible.

Choose large or small journals depending on your subject, and smooth paper for image transfers and sketches in ink and pencil; for watercolor, gouache, and acrylic paints, you will need watercolor sketchbooks or journals with thick handmade paper. Journal covers and even spines can be collaged. If you plan to leave any of those surfaces uncovered, choose colors and patterns that will go with your subject.

Papers for collage include vintage and antique ephemera found in secondhand stores and antique stores, as well as at flea markets and paper fairs, along with scrap art (widely available on the Internet and in books), and of course your own photos, letters, and mementos such as old tickets, menus, and maps.

Different kinds of closure devices are a charming addition to collage journals, including ribbons, buttons, string ties, and vintage belt buckles. You can also add your own ribbon page markers or add ornaments to existing ones, or place loose markers, such as feathers or bookmarks, inside the journals.

Notebook binders with plastic pocket sleeves are a great way to store and protect collage scrap art and paper ephemera until ready for use.

A wide variety of materials can be used for collage journals, from decorative papers and vintage ephemera to ribbons, buttons, and buckles used as interesting closure devices.

PAPERS

Decorative and handmade papers

Alphabet stickers

Antique and vintage wallpaper

Wine labels

Antique and vintage ephemera:
maps, letters, music scores,
postal stamps, scrap art, prints,
postcards, etc.

Reproductions of antique and
vintage cards, letters, etc.

Journals

Shipping tags

Printed paper napkins

Labels

Photo corners

Decorative paper leaves

Waxed paper

MISCELLANEOUS

Ribbons and fabric trim

Buttons

Antique belt buckles

Feathers

Glassine envelopes

Plant tags

Pressed botanicals

{ Travel Journals }

Travel Journals, one of the most satisfying kinds of illustrated books, naturally lend themselves to collage. Postcards, pages from travel guides, photographs, and vintage ephemera found in shops and outdoor markets on your travels are keepsakes that evoke the place where they originated and memorialize the trip. The same materials can be used to create an imaginary travel journal of a place you've always wanted to see but haven't yet visited, as in the Africa Dream Journal on this page.

Africa Dream Journal

This dream journal, based on an itinerary from a travel guide, has a cover painted with rubbed-on acrylic paint. The image of entwined leaves and twigs was transferred from a Dover book, and the lion was painted on top. The "D'Afrique" label in the lower right-hand corner is from a set of cards. The seal was made with sealing wax and a letter stamp.

PAINTING TECHNIQUE

The book used for this dream journal has heavy handmade paper with deckled edges that gives it the look of an old journal. Each page was coated with a wash of acrylic paint before being written on with an imagined account of an African journey and illustrated with watercolor animal sketches.

COLLAGE TECHNIQUE

Left-hand page: Two images of a cheetah were painted on the page and notes of an imagined sighting of the cat were added in Walnut Stain ink. Tissue paper printed in a cheetah-fur pattern was torn and pasted on top of the acrylic-washed pages.

The top layer of a paper napkin, printed with the image of a cheetah, was separated from the bottom two layers. The central image was torn from the printed layer and pasted on top of the tissue paper. *(See page 68 on collaging with paper napkins.)*

MATERIALS

Journal with heavy handmade paper and deckled edges, "Cheetah" paper napkin, "Cheetah fur" tissue paper, assorted decorative papers in animal and African prints, antique wallpaper, Cavallini & Company postcard, D'Afrique gift cards, Yes! paste, Buff Titanium acrylic paint, Van Dyke Brown or Burnt Sienna watercolor for edging, assorted watercolors for animal sketches, white gouache, Walnut Stain ink, calligraphy pen, paste brush, heavy book, sealing wax and "M" seal, paper-covered brick

PROCESS

1. Paint several pages of the journal at a time with a thin wash of Titanium Buff acrylic paint.

2. While the paper is still wet, brush the deckled edges of the painted pages with Van Dyke Brown or Burnt Sienna watercolor.

3. Using Walnut Stain ink, write an imagined account of a journey to Africa on several pages.

4. Illustrate some of the handwritten pages with watercolor sketches.

5. Using Yes! paste, cover some pages with torn pieces of African-print paper or animal-print tissue paper.

6. Superimpose African postcards and torn sheets of separated layers of paper napkins illustrated with a cheetah on top of the paper-covered pages.

COLLAGE TECHNIQUE

A nineteenth-century French document, a torn piece of decorative paper, and African stamps were pasted on an old postcard, shown on the left-hand page. Bird eggs were painted on the card using gouache *(see page 29 for painting eggs technique);* the card was then scumbled with gouache and allowed to dry.

The card was sprayed with fixative and mounted on the previously scumbled and edged journal page using gold self-adhesive photo corners. A guinea feather from Africa was placed in the center of the journal. Quick watercolor sketches were painted on the right-hand page, which was then pasted with African stamps and labeled in Walnut Stain ink.

MATERIALS

Antique French document, vintage postcard (address side), marbled paper, decorative paper, stamps, watercolors and gouache (and brushes), oxgall, fixative, acrylics, Walnut Stain ink, Derwent sketching pencil (dark wash), scumbling brush, gold self-adhesive photo corners

PAINTING TECHNIQUE

1. Draw birds and eggs on the previously scumbled and edged page using the Derwent sketching pencil.

2. Using watercolors, and white gouache for opaque areas, paint in the birds quickly to give a spontaneous, painted-on-site look.

3. Affix the stamps and add text using the calligraphy pen and Walnut Stain ink.

PAINTING TECHNIQUE:
HOW TO PAINT EGGS WITH GOUACHE

Gouache is a water-based paint that is rich in pigment, which makes it more opaque and light-reflective than watercolor. Gouache is a quick and effective way to add color to collages, whether you want to highlight some printed element or add new images like these eggs. All you need is a set of gouache paints and a few inexpensive watercolor brushes. The illustrations here show how to embellish your collage works with eggs.

1. Draw the egg outline with a light pencil.

2. Using gouache, paint in a base coat of Yellow Ochre, Permanent White, and a small amount of Indigo Blue.

3. Use oxgall instead of water to blend in Permanent White over base coat. Highlight with Permanent White.

4. Cut a template of the egg out of tracing paper and place it on the egg. Using a stencil brush, splatter in small spots with Burnt Sienna. Remove the template. Using a small, pointed brush, paint more spots on the edges of the egg.

5. Using the side of a brush, paint in large spots and scrawls with Burnt Sienna and very light Spectrum Violet. Add darker spots and scrawls with Van Dyke Brown.

6. Create a shadow with Indigo Blue along the edges. Let dry completely.

7. Cover the egg with a Cream 914 Berol pencil, then scrape with an X-acto knife. Shadow the bottom edge with pencil. Highlight the center with dry-brushed Permanent White. Cover the highlight with white pencil, then scrape with an X-acto knife.

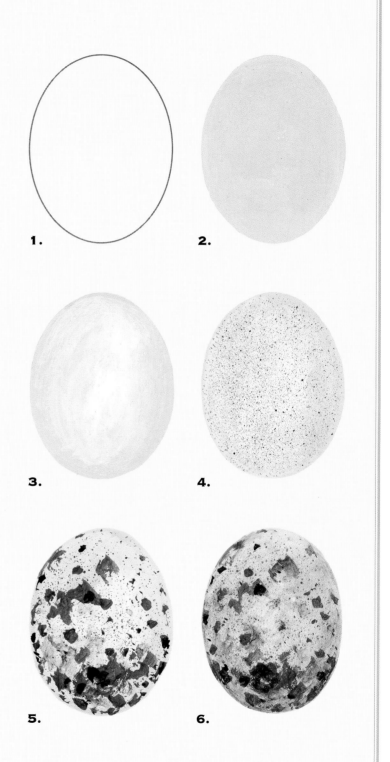

1.   2.

3.   4.

5.   6.

Venice Sketchbook Journal ☞

Gift cards, decorative paper, and ephemera purchased on a trip to Venice, along with other souvenirs, all found their way into the collages in this journal. Here, collaged pieces of characters from commedia dell'arte are combined with watercolor sketches to give the journal a lyrical feeling throughout. A bill from the Villa Pitiana was attached to a left-hand page and used as the ground for a sketch of the exterior of the villa; the facing page has details of the interior walls of the villa and artist's notes listing the specific gouache colors used for the sketches.

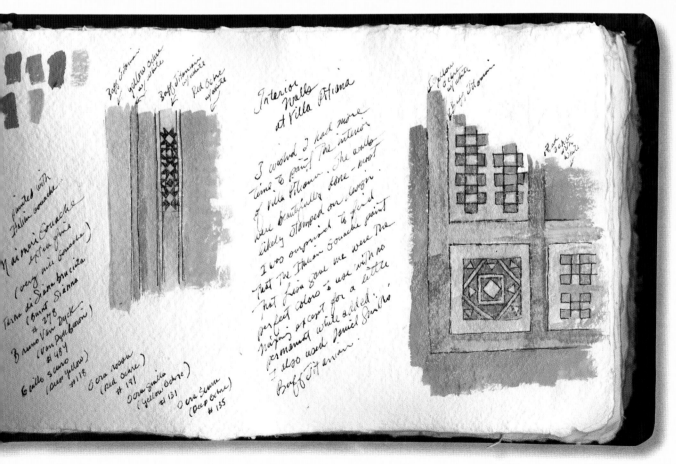

Il Ponte di Rialto

CANOVA S.A.S.
DI BUSATO F. & C.
SAN MARCO 701
VENEZIA

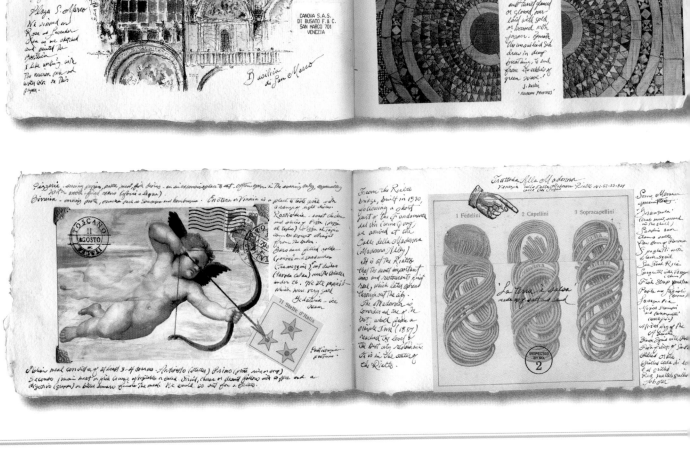

COLLAGE TECHNIQUE

Sketches were made with a .005 Micron black pen, then painted over with watercolor. Gift cards were decorated with postage stamps and rubber stamps of postage cancellations; quotes from famous visitors to Venice were then written on the cards with Walnut Stain ink. The cards were mounted on the journal pages with self-adhesive decorative gold corners. A piece of a poster illustrated with different kinds of pasta was pasted on, stamped with rubber stamps, and inked with an Italian proverb. Journal notes of the trip were then written in.

My dear fellow, nothing in the world that ever you have heard of Venice, is equal to the magnificent and stupendous reality. The wildest visions of The Arabian Nights are nothing to the piazza of Saint Mark, and the impression of the inside of the church. The gorgeous and wonderful reality of Venice is beyond the fancy of the wildest dreamer. Opium couldn't build such a place, and enchantment couldn't shadow it forth in a vision. All that I have heard of it, read of it in truth or fiction, fancied of it, is left thousands of miles behind! You know that I am liable to disappointment in such things from over-expectation, but Venice is above, beyond, out of all reach coming near, the first sensation of man......

CHARLES DICKENS

Extract from a letter written to his friend John Forster – November 12, 1844

S. Giorgio Maggiore - Venezia

A gondolier gliding by the Santa Maria della Salute

Santa Maria della Salute stands at the entrance of the Grand Canal. Henry James described it as "some great lady on the threshold of her salon." It was built in thanksgiving for the city's deliverance from the plague epidemic of 1630 – hence the name 'Salute' meaning health and Salvation. Baldassare Longhena started building the church in 1630 at the age of 32 – he worked on it for the rest of his life! It was not completed until 1687 – 5 years after his death.

Sketching Santa Maria della Salute. The root weight of this Baroque church is supported by over one million timber piles.

Detail of one of the colossal scrolls that disguise the buttresses

Hawaii
Hawaii falls just inside the
eastern tip of the Indo-Pacific
Province.
The reefs around the Hawaiian
Islands are like those of the West
Atlantic. The islands
are surrounded with
terraces of
rubble,
some corals
and
and a fine
of mollusks suited to
this habitat. We found lots of
coral rubble — large and small pieces in
all forms with lovely shades of whites, pinks, roots and
blues. It was a beautiful contrast to the black lava that
shored the sandy rocky beaches.
Hawaii

There were three kinds of coral reefs: fringing reefs,

barrier reefs, and encircling reefs–and so

№ 3.

Coraux Rouges

Hawaiian Travel Journal

A little pocket-sized journal was chosen for a trip to the Big Island because it was small enough to carry around for quick sketch painting and collaging. The cover was pasted with decorative paper cut to follow the contour of the cover and leave the black border of the journal exposed. A turtle cut from an antique advertising card was painted on with acrylic and inscribed in Walnut Stain ink, then mounted on black paper and pasted on the cover. A decorative label was labeled in ink for the title page, and a millinery fabric leaf was attached to the journal's ribbon page marker. Decorative papers and paper napkins printed with shells were used for collaged pages.

Italy Journal

The cover and many of the pages of this travel journal were prepared before a trip to Italy, leaving blank areas for writing. Antique postcards, rubber stamps, labels, image transfers, and a glassine envelope were used to make this journal evocative of Italy. The Italian stamps were purchased on the trip and added to the journal later.

COLLAGE TECHNIQUE

Top two pages: A vintage postcard was attached to scumbled journal pages with photo corners, and the card was stamped with a rubber cancellation stamp. A large postage stamp and a scrap art clown were added. The text was written during the trip using a .005 Micron black pen.

PROCESS

1. Scumble the pages of the journal, with watercolors and gouache. *(See page 41 for scumbling painting technique.)*

2. Lower left-hand pages: Paste the olive oil label with the image of a face on the page and scumble with paint; stamp with "No. 500" using a rubber stamp; stamp the eye of the face on the label with a rubber stamp of an eye.

3. Right-hand page: Paste on an antique map of Florence, folded so that it can be opened out; scumble the outside of the map with watercolors and gouache; let dry, then paste a vintage label on the map and rubber-stamp it with the Roman numerals and the word *Fiorenza*. Paste on the Dresden dove and brush with brown watercolor.

4. Upper left-hand page: Paste in the wine label; paste Italian stamps on the label and its edges; add a cancellation mark using a rubber stamp.

5. Journal pages, above: Paste the left-hand page with a large Italian stamp and write in details of a trip to the Italian countryside in black ink around it.

6. Paste the right-hand page with an antique hand-painted card of a picnic basket. Affix a ribbon bow above the card using a brass brad, and glue a fragment of a sunflower wax seal to the bow. Attach decorative leaf to the right side of the page by punching holes through the page with an awl, then inserting the stem (paste a label on the back of the page to hide the holes).

NO. 500

IRIDESCENT COPPER
QUINACRIDONE
BURNT ORANGE
WHITE
YELLOW OCHRE
PERSIAN
RED

PAINTING TECHNIQUE:
HOW TO SCUMBLE JOURNAL PAGES

Scumbling is the technique of applying a thin, uneven coat of paint with an almost-dry brush; used on collages and journal pages, it adds a layer of color that allows the paper underneath it to show through, giving it the aged look of an antique fresco or a fading painted plaster wall. Scumbling the white pages of a blank journal gives the book a vintage look and helps the collage work blend in.

1. Paste paper ephemera, in this case an olive oil label with a Renaissance painting of a face, in the center of the page. Weight with the paper-covered brick and let dry. Place a sheet of paper towel between the page you wish to scumble and the page beneath it to protect the preceding pages and journal cover when scumbling.

2. Using a scumbling brush to approximate the uneven painted surfaces of fading frescoes and walls in Italy, dry-brush Daniel Smith Iridescent Copper watercolor right from the tube, using no water, on the page. In the same way, scumble Permanent White gouache lightly over the page, then add Quinacridone Burnt Orange, then more Permanent White. Scumble over the label and around the edges to give the label the same patina as the background page.

3. Scumble more layers of colors such as Yellow Ochre, more Permanent White, and Persian Red, letting the colors underneath show through. Use the scumbling brush to blend the colors unevenly.

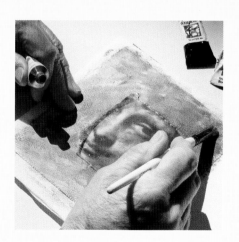

Poulardes de Bresse Truffées

(Roast Chicken with Truffles)

Bresse is famous for their poultry — free range chickens.
Poularde is a plump mature chicken with more flavor than
a poulet.

MIRABELLE
DE
LORRAINE

50°   D

MIRABELLE BRANDY
4/5 QUART   PRODUCE OF FRANCE

COOPÉRATIVE DES PRODUCTEURS DE MIRABELLES DE LORRAINE
TANTONVILLE · M·&·M · FRANCE

Roast chicken same as recipe for roasting pheasant.
Insert truffles under the skin instead of covering with
slices of bacon. Rub outside of skin with butter.
1/2 hour before done, pour brandy over the chicken.
When done, rest chicken for 20 minutes — then pour
pan drippings with brandy over the chicken.

{ Food & Wine Journals }

~

Food & Wine Journals are perfect keepsakes for lovers of food and wine to give, to receive, or to add to their own library. A journal commemorating a meal or celebration makes a unique and charming thank-you gift for a host, and is a lasting token for the honored guest of any special event, such as a wedding or anniversary dinner. A collection of recipes is another gift that food-loving friends will appreciate. And an illustrated food or wine journal is a lovely way for hosts to record every detail of a favorite event.

👉 *Wine Journal*

Vintage wine labels and advertising cards for wines are collaged in this little book to make a gift that anyone who loves wine would cherish. But wine-lovers could also use this journal as a model for an artful way to collect the labels of favorite wines for future reference or as mementos of special occasions.

👉 *French Recipe Journal*

This journal was created around a set of early-twentieth-century French menu cards found in an antique shop. The pages of a blank photo album were collaged with antique French postcards, maps, wine labels, and other ephemera. Classic French recipes were hand-written on facing pages. The cover was pasted with flocked paper, and an antique blank French menu card was used as a title frame.

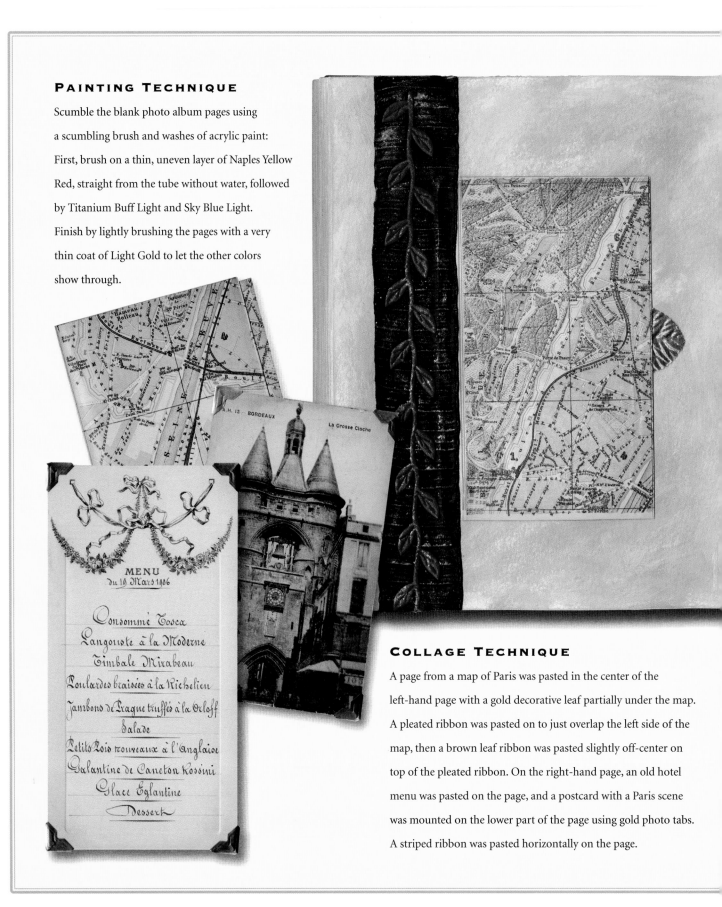

PAINTING TECHNIQUE

Scumble the blank photo album pages using
a scumbling brush and washes of acrylic paint:
First, brush on a thin, uneven layer of Naples Yellow
Red, straight from the tube without water, followed
by Titanium Buff Light and Sky Blue Light.
Finish by lightly brushing the pages with a very
thin coat of Light Gold to let the other colors
show through.

COLLAGE TECHNIQUE

A page from a map of Paris was pasted in the center of the
left-hand page with a gold decorative leaf partially under the map.
A pleated ribbon was pasted on to just overlap the left side of the
map, then a brown leaf ribbon was pasted slightly off-center on
top of the pleated ribbon. On the right-hand page, an old hotel
menu was pasted on the page, and a postcard with a Paris scene
was mounted on the lower part of the page using gold photo tabs.
A striped ribbon was pasted horizontally on the page.

PROCESS

1. Left-hand page: Paste the folded map of Paris on the scumbled page by placing a line of paste on the left side of the map and affixing it. Paste the wide ribbon over that edge, down the left side of the page. Brush the ribbon lightly with Brilliant Gold gouache. Paste the leaf ribbon in the center of the wide ribbon. Paste one half of the decorative leaf on the last folded page inside the map to use as a pull. Weight with the paper-covered brick until dry.

2. Right-hand page: Fold up the bottom 2¾ inches of the New Hotel menu and paste the top part of the menu to the journal page. Weight with a heavy book until the paste is dry. Scumble the same colors that were used on the journal page on the folded-up section of the menu. Paste the striped ribbon to the top edge of this folded section. Weight with the paper-covered brick until dry.

3. Apply gold self-adhesive photo corners to the antique postcard. Affix the top edge of the postcard to the menu and the bottom edge to the journal page. Attach the leaf ribbon to the top left corner of the journal page by punching a hole in the page with the Japanese screw punch and threading the ribbon through, then tying it to the page.

MATERIALS

Pleated ribbon (1½ inches wide), brown leaf ribbon, striped ribbon, folded map of Paris from an early-twentieth-century edition of Baedeker's *Paris and Its Environs,* gold decorative leaf, 1840 menu from the New Hotel in Cairo, antique Paris postcard, Yes! paste, gold self-adhesive photo corners, scumbling brush, Amsterdam acrylic paints (Naples Yellow Red, Titanium Buff Light, Sky Blue Light, Light Gold), Brilliant Gold gouache, filbert brush, paste brush, paper-covered brick

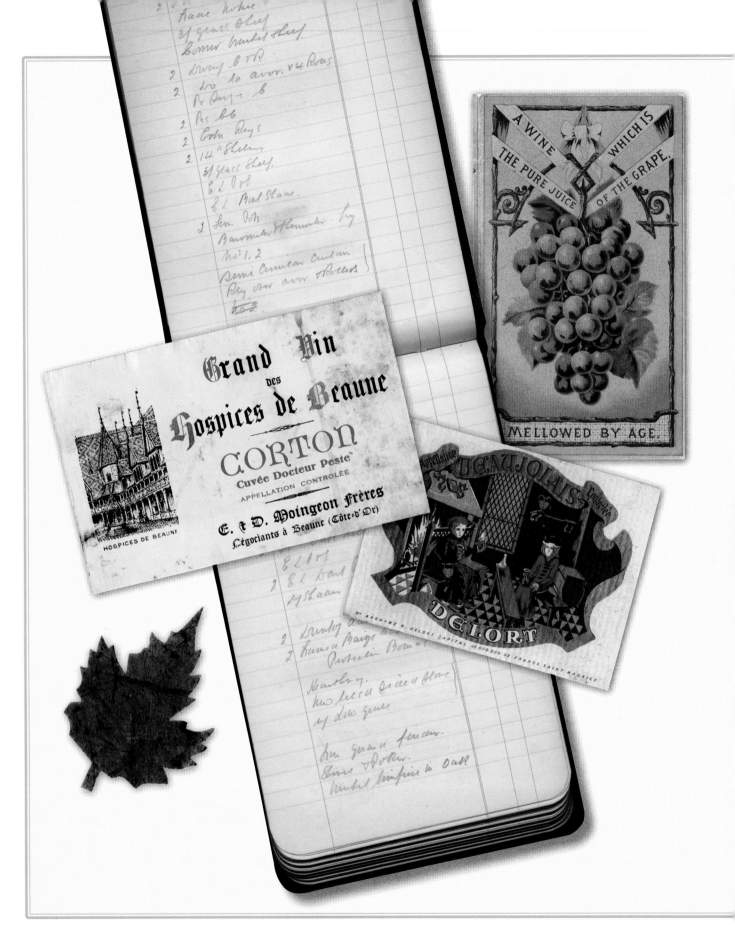

Wine Journal

Wine-lovers who save the labels of particularly favored bottles of wine (or collectors of ephemera, who value the designs of wine labels) can keep them in a wine journal like this one, made from a small antique hotel logbook from England. Fittingly, the leather-bound cover is the same color as a wonderful claret. The wine labels were pasted in the logbook to leave some of the original handwritten notations exposed. An antique advertising card for Underhill wine was pasted on the cover, then topped with the vintage brass bow from a shoe and a round label with the title of the journal written in Walnut Stain ink.

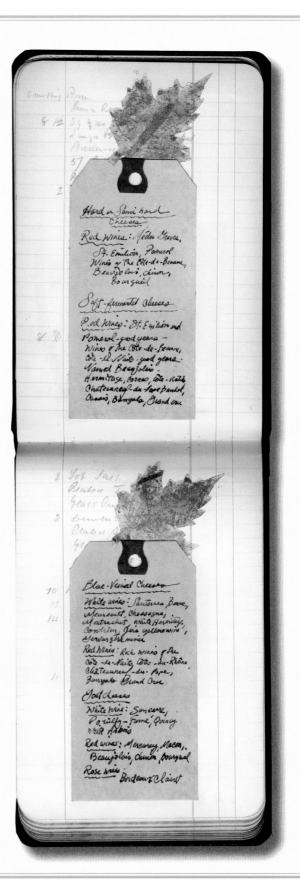

COLLAGE TECHNIQUE

Far-left journal pages: The cut-out paper leaves were brushed with Brilliant Gold gouache. A section of the antique map of France was pasted on the bottom page. The wine label was pasted on top, then topped with one of the painted paper leaves. The self-adhesive label was affixed to the leaf and labeled with Walnut Stain ink. Notes on Underhill wine were added to the top page. Near-left pages: A gold-brushed paper leaf was pasted at the top of each page. Antique shipping tags were pasted on the top and bottom pages,

partially overlapping the leaves and leaving some of the original logbook entries exposed. Pairings of wines and cheeses were written on the shipping tags with Walnut Stain ink. This page, above: The image of birds at table was pasted on the antique French place card on the bottom of the page, and a gold-brushed leaf was pasted on to partially overlap the gift card. A self-adhesive label was affixed to the leaf, and the section title was written on it with Walnut Stain ink.

MATERIALS

Antique English hotel logbook, round labels, decorative paper leaves, antique wine labels, small antique playing card with Champagne bottle image, antique photo of a woman christening a ship, antique advertising card for Underhill wine, portion of antique French map, old shipping tags, small antique French place card with bird images, stamp with grape image, Brilliant Gold gouache, Yes! paste, paste brush, Walnut Stain ink, calligraphy pen, .005 Micron black pen, paper-covered brick

PROCESS

1. Far-left journal pages: Paste the wine label on the top page, then paste a portion of an antique photo of a woman christening a ship on top of the label. Add the cutout portion of a stamp with a grape image and ink in vine curls along the edge. Weight with the paper-covered brick and let dry.

2. For the lower page: Paste in the small playing card image of a Champagne bottle. Brush Brilliant Gold gouache over the decorative paper leaf, then paste the leaf on the page with the bottom portion of the leaf overlapping the playing card. Paste the round label on the leaf and write *Wine* on the label with Walnut Stain ink.

3. Central journal pages: Paste the Underhill wine advertising card on the top page and top with the round label. Weight with the paper-covered brick and let dry. Write *Notes* on the label with Walnut Stain ink. Copy the notes from the advertising card onto the bottom page with the .005 Micron black pen.

4. Near-left journal pages: Paste the wine labels on the upper and lower pages. Brush the decorative paper leaves with Brilliant Gold gouache. Paste the leaves partially over the labels. Weight with the paper-covered brick and let dry.

Favorite Desserts

⬥ *Dessert Journal*

A journal of favorite desserts was given a chocolate brown self-adhesive cloth binding; marbled paper was then pasted on the front and back covers. A huge strawberry, cut from wrapping paper, was pasted on the front. For the title, a label was edged with Brilliant Gold gouache, then pasted on and labeled with Walnut Stain ink. A vintage hand cutout was pasted partly on top and a green velvet ribbon fastened with a vintage buckle was wrapped around the journal. The interior was collaged with pages and cutouts from vintage dessert booklets from gelatin and chocolate producers, bridge tally cards, paper napkins, scraps of antique wallpaper, scrap art, an antique soap label, and fruit and sacks of flour cut from advertising cards; the recipes were written in using Walnut Stain ink.

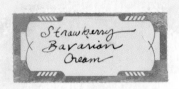

Strawberry
Bavarian
Cream

¼ box Knox Gelatine (KNOX SPARKLING)
¼ cup cold water
1 cup strawberry juice and pulp

Juice of half a lemon
½ cup sugar
1½ cups double cream beaten solid

Soften the gelatine in the cold water five minutes and let dissolve by standing in hot water; strain into the strawberry and lemon juice; add the sugar and stir until it is dissolved, then set into ice water and stir until the mixture begins to thicken; fold in the chilled cream. Turn into a mold lined with strawberries cut in halves, and when chilled turn from the mold. Garnish with fresh berries and leaves. Prepare Bavarian creams with other fruits, as pineapple, raspberry, grapes, oranges, etc, in the same manner. Pineapple juice and pulp must be scalded before the gelatine is added to it, for if this is not done the acid of the fresh pineapple will digest the gelatine so that it will not harden.

PAINTING TECHNIQUE: TINTING BACKGROUND PAGES

Tinting the pages allows you to create a special color palette for your journal, depending on the subject of your book and the overall look you want. A light tint also adds interest to journals with white or cream pages, gives the journal as a whole a vintage appearance, and creates visual unity throughout the book.

1. Using a scumbling brush, paint the borders of several pages at a time with Naples Yellow Red acrylic.

2. Vary some pages by scumbling a little Transparent Red Medium acrylic or Persian Rose acrylic over the Naples Yellow Red.

3. Scumble Titanium Buff Light acrylic over the painted borders, extending it into the center of the page to create a darker border and a lighter center on each page.

NO OTHER FOOD PRODUCT
HAS A LIKE RECORD.

ESTABLISHED 1780.

57 HIGHEST AWARDS.

CHOCOLATE PARFAIT.
(See Page 28.)

CHOCOLATE ÉCLAIRS.
(See Page 17.)

CHOCOLATE LAYER CAKE.
(See Page 28.)

WALTER BAKER & CO.'S
GERMAN'S
SWEET CHOCOLATE

GERMAN'S SWEET CHOCOLATE

FAC-SIMILE ¼ LB. PACKAGE.

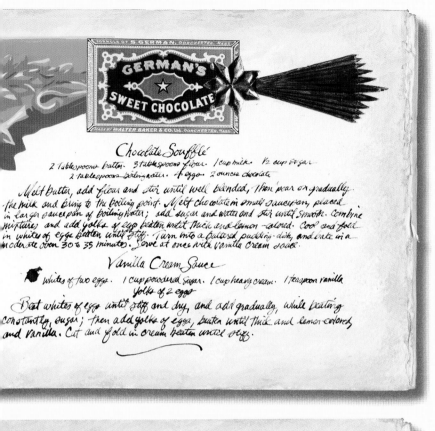

Chocolate Soufflé

2 Tablespoons butter. 3 Tablespoons flour. 1 cup milk. ½ cup sugar.
2 tablespoons boiling water. 4 eggs. 2 ounces chocolate.

Melt butter, add flour and stir until well blended, then pour on gradually the milk and bring to the boiling point. Melt chocolate in small saucepan, placed in larger saucepan of boiling water; add sugar and water and stir until smooth. Combine mixtures and add yolks of eggs beaten until thick and lemon-colored. Cool and fold in whites of eggs beaten until stiff. Turn into a buttered pudding-dish, and bake in a moderate oven 30 to 35 minutes. Serve at once with Vanilla Cream Sauce.

Vanilla Cream Sauce

whites of two eggs. 1 cup powdered sugar. 1 cup heavy cream. 1 teaspoon vanilla
yolks of 2 eggs

Beat whites of eggs until stiff and dry, and add gradually, while beating constantly, sugar; then add yolks of eggs, beaten until thick and lemon-colored and vanilla. Cut and fold in cream beaten until stiff.

Chocolate Parfait

1 quart heavy cream. 3 squares chocolate.
1 cup sugar. 2 teaspoons vanilla.

Put into the upper part of a double-boiler half cup of milk; when hot add chocolate and mix until chocolate is melted. Then add sugar. Sift this in pan of cold water, and as it cools add the cream slowly at first until mixture is smooth. Add vanilla and enough sugar to make quite sweet. Beat mixture until stiff. Turn into a large mould, pack in ice and salt and let it stand at least two hours.

Chocolate Parfait

Chocolate Oysterettes

Oyster crackers, salted preferred. ½ pound semi sweet
3 baskets of figs cut very small chocolate

Select fresh-baked crackers free from crumbs. Melt semi-sweet chocolate in a small double-boiler. The inner dish of the boiler should be of such size that the melted chocolate will come nearly to the top of it. Cool melted chocolate to 80°F. Drop cracker into the chocolate, with a fork pick it below the chocolate, lift out and drop onto waxed paper. Do not let a drop of water get into chocolate. Add figs to the chocolate used for dipping if you like.

Chocolate Oysterettes plain and with chopped figs.

Chocolate Éclairs

½ cup butter. 1 cup milk. 2 Tablespoons sugar. 4 eggs. 1 cup flour.
Put butter, milk and sugar into saucepan. Bring to the boiling point, add flour all at once and stir vigorously using a wooden spoon. Remove from stove as soon as mixture cleaves to spoon. Cool, add flour, eggs, one at a time, beating two minutes between the addition of each egg and four minutes after eggs are added. (cont. on next page)

Chocolate Éclairs

Top journal pages: The cover and illustrations cut from a vintage chocolate recipe book were used to collage a section on chocolate desserts in this journal. First, a design on a piece of wallpaper was cut out to extend from the left-hand page to part of the right-hand page, then cut in half to leave the gutter of the book free; the pieces were pasted at the top of each page. The German's Sweet Chocolate label was pasted over the end of wallpaper on the right-hand page. A Dresden tassel ornament was brushed with Walnut Stain ink to age it, then pasted to the right of the chocolate label. The image of the woman serving chocolate was pasted on the left side of the page, partially overlapping the wallpaper. The strip of chocolate brown ribbon was pasted on the bottom of the left-hand page, and the recipes were written in with Walnut Stain ink. Bottom journal pages: The cover of the chocolate booklet was pasted on the left-hand page. Cutout pictures of chocolate desserts from the booklet were pasted at the bottom and sides of the pages, and the recipes were written in around them using Walnut Stain ink.

MATERIALS

Vintage dessert booklet (*Dainty Desserts for Dainty People*, from Knox Gelatine), vintage gold doily, vintage tiny doily, brocade ribbon, candy label adornment, ribbon, vintage scrap rose, gold self-adhesive photo corners, antique card of fruit, Dresden ornament, .005 Micron black pen, Walnut Stain ink, calligraphy pen, Yes! paste, paste brush, paper-covered brick

PROCESS

1. Tint the background of all the pages in the book (*see page 57*) a few pages at a time.

2. Top journal pages: Paste cutout images from the vintage dessert booklet on the left side of the page; weight down with the paper-covered brick and let dry. Paste the Dresden ornament at the top of the right-hand page; weight and let dry. Write in the recipes using a .005 Micron black pen; add the titles using Walnut Stain ink.

3. Paste the cutout decorative image from the dessert booklet on the top of the right-hand page and paste the tiny doily to the right. Paste the image of the woman on top. Cut the brocade ribbon twice the width of the page and paste the first half horizontally on the page. Paste on the candy label, overlapping the ribbon slightly. Weight with the paper-covered brick and let dry.

4. Bottom journal pages: Paste the other half of the brocade ribbon on the back of the preceding page; weight down with the paper-covered brick and let dry. Paste the small ribbon down the seam of the journal. Paste the gold doily, gold side down, on the upper corner of the left-hand page. Paste an antique scrap art rose on top of the doily; weight with the paper-covered brick until dry.

5. Mount the antique card of fruit on the right-hand page using self-adhesive gold photo borders. Write in the recipes on both pages using Walnut Stain ink.

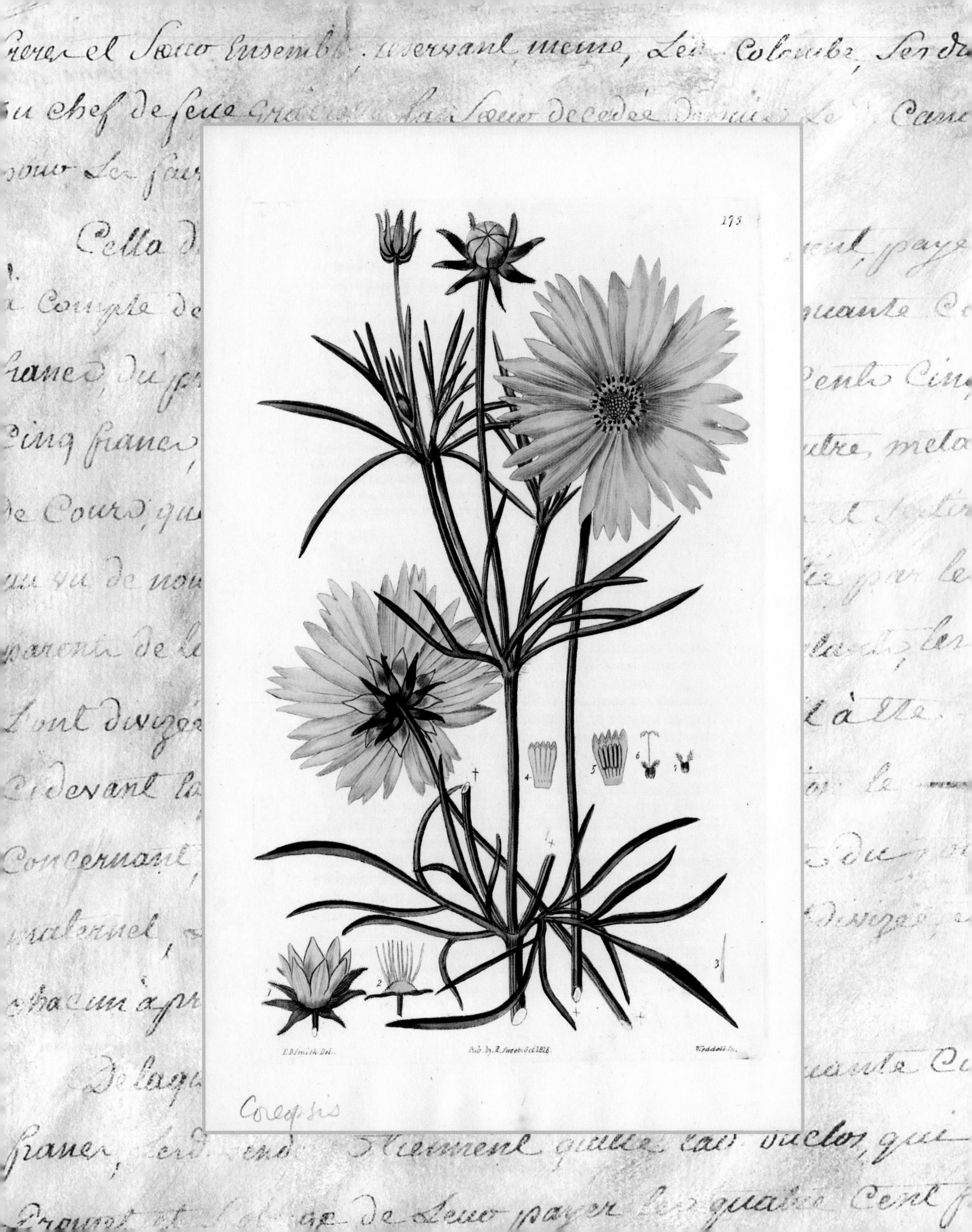
175
E.D.Smith Del.
Pub. by R. Sweet. Oct 1826.
Coreopsis

{ Nature & Garden Journals }

Nature & Garden Journals are a prized way to record the life of a garden or the passage of the seasons. Botanical studies of flora and fauna may have been the original inspiration for these kinds of journals, but amateur gardeners and nature-lovers have long been drawn to celebrating the natural beauty of the world around them. A rich array of nature-themed ephemera, along with pressed botanicals and original drawings, makes these illustrated journals bloom.

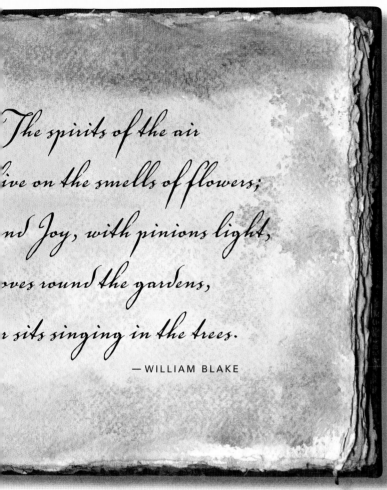

The spirits of the air
live on the smells of flowers;
nd Joy, with pinions light,
ves round the gardens,
r sits singing in the trees.

— WILLIAM BLAKE

Garden Poetry Journal

A collection of poems and lines of poetry about birds and flowers, collaged with antique floral wallpaper and images of birds, makes a lovely gift for any lover of both poetry and gardens.

Nature Journal ☞

Collaged nature journals can be small books with one subject, such as dragonflies or one specific place in nature, or a record of the passage of time in the natural world, from one day to one season or an entire year. The cover of this little book, created from a new cloth-covered blank journal, is collaged with a pressed leaf and a Dresden dragonfly.

Hawaiian Nature Journal

A blank spiral-bound artist's sketchbook with rough-textured cold-press watercolor paper was used for this nature journal of Hawaii. A heavy oilclothlike paper was folded over the cover of the book, then collaged with decorative paper, printed paper napkins, a piece of vintage sheet of music, and a self-adhesive label. A stretch ribbon was wrapped around the journal, and a fabric "frog" closure was attached to the bow.

MATERIALS

Watercolor sketch book, decorative paper, vintage music score "Hawaiian Rose," decorative label, paper napkin with pineapple image, paper napkin with magnolia image, decorative marbled rice paper, Brilliant Gold gouache, Yes! paste, heavy book, paste brush, filbert brush for applying gouache

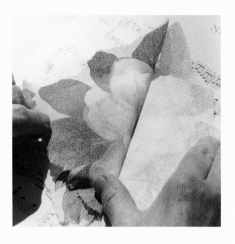

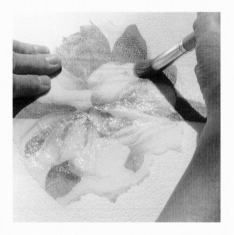

Collage Technique: Collage with Paper Napkins

Paper napkins, which come printed in a wide assortment of patterns and illustrations, are a good way to add visual interest to journal pages and to carry through a theme. They usually have three layers, the printed top layer and two solid-color bottom layers. When the printed top sheet is used for collage, it adds an intriguing semitransparent layer to the page.

1. First, create and paste down the background art, here an old piece of sheet music pasted on marbled paper.

2. Carefully remove the printed top layer from the bottom two layers of each of the paper napkins; discard the bottom layers. Tear the printed layers of each napkin to leave the portion of the image you want. Place the image face down on waxed paper. Carefully apply paste in the center of the napkin (take care not to tear the delicate paper), using outward brushstrokes from the center to cover the entire image.

3. Carefully peel the image from the waxed paper and place face up on the background art. Smooth out the wrinkles with your hand. Using a damp paper towel, dab away any excess paste. If using another image, repeat the process, placing it on top of the first image.

4. Place a sheet of waxed paper over the napkin images. Weight with the heavy book and let dry.

COLLAGE TECHNIQUE

Left-hand page: A torn sheet of marbled paper was pasted on the page. The top layer of a paper napkin was separated from the bottom two layers; the image of the palm trees was then torn from the top layer and pasted on the page. *(See the collage with paper napkin technique on page 68.)*

The antique coconut advertising card was pasted on top of the decorative paper, then the scrap art bird on a nest was pasted on to partially cover the advertising card. A rocky beach was painted in watercolor on the right-hand page.

MATERIALS

Large journal with handmade paper, decorative paper, paper napkin with palm tree image, advertising card for concentrated coconut, scrap art bird on nest, watercolors and brushes, Yes! paste, heavy book, paper-covered brick, paste brush, Walnut Stain ink, calligraphy pen

COLLAGE TECHNIQUE

Left-hand page: Seedpods were painted in watercolor and labeled with Walnut Stain ink using the calligraphy pen; notes were added on where the seedpods were found. Right-hand page: A strip of decorative paper was pasted on the left side of the page. The antique postcard was scumbled with gouache and allowed to dry, then pasted on the page, overlapping the decorative paper.

A fragment of a stamp with palm trees was pasted on the bottom of the postcard; rubber stamps of palm trees were added, and a watercolor wash was applied to the trees. Text was written in using Walnut Stain ink and the calligraphy pen. Lower right-hand journal page: Palm trees were painted in using watercolors. A decorative antique card was pasted on the right side of the page. Lines of poetry were written in

using Walnut Stain ink. The Hawaii postage stamp was pasted on the bottom, and a cancellation mark was added with a rubber stamp. Top right-hand journal page: Decorative paper was pasted on the page, and the advertising card with a boy and girl on the beach was pasted on top. A fragment of scrap art (the sailboat) was pasted on the bottom, and the poetry quote was added using Walnut Stain ink.

MATERIALS

Large journal with handmade paper, decorative papers, antique postcard, rubber stamp of palm trees and inkpad, rubber stamp with Hawaii cancellation, postage stamp, antique advertising card, small decorative antique card with beach scene image, Walnut Stain ink, calligraphy pen, watercolors and brushes, heavy book, paper-covered brick, Yes! paste, paste brush

SPADE, THE GARDENER.

COLLAGE TECHNIQUE

For the cover: The natural brown cover of the journal was brushed with Light Gold acrylic. The decorative red paper was pasted on, then weighted and allowed to dry. The square of antique floral wallpaper was pasted over the decorative paper. The edges of the antique advertising card ("Spade, the Gardener") was brushed with Brilliant Gold gouache, then pasted on top of the wallpaper.

MATERIALS

Artist's watercolor sketchbook with heavy brown cover and heavy handmade brown paper, photo of gardeners from the Museum of Garden History in London, photos of Monet and his garden in Giverny, ticket to Renoir's garden, copper plant tag, tag alphabet stickers, pressed flowers and leaves, floral-themed postage stamps, transparent tape, watercolors and brushes, rubber-stamp numerals and ink pad, .005 Micron black pen, Yes! paste, paste brush

Garden Sketchbook Journal

Dedicated gardeners can keep a journal of their garden year by drawing or painting on-site watercolor sketches and combining them with collaged garden-themed ephemera, seed packets, and pressed flowers and leaves from the garden. This journal, made from a watercolor sketchbook, has a painted gold cover pasted with plant-themed decorative paper, vintage wallpaper, and an advertising card of a gardener.

COLLAGE TECHNIQUE

Top left pages: The left-hand page was painted with a field of lavender in watercolor and labeled with a .005 Micron black pen. The photo of the gardeners was pasted on the right-hand page. A hole was made in the top of the page with an awl and the copper plant tag attached to the top of the page by twisting the wire on the back of the page. "Garden Journal" was added using old price tags, rubber-stamped with the capital letters, and the black pen.

Bottom right pages: A ticket to Renoir's garden in Cagnes-sur-Mer, France, was pasted on the left-hand page. A watercolor sketch of Renoir's olive trees was pasted on the right-hand page, and dried pressed flowers and grass from Renoir's garden were affixed to the page with transparent tape. The page number was rubber-stamped in the upper right-hand corner, and text added with the black pen.

Dried botanicals—including flowers, leaves, moss, and seeds—are exquisite materials for collage. If pressed and preserved correctly, they will last indefinitely and retain much of their color inside a journal.

PRESSING BOTANICALS TECHNIQUE

Using botanicals adds intricacy, beauty, and uniqueness to a journal. And this technique also allows you to preserve natural materials that are special mementos or meaningful to you by incorporating them into a collage.

Make sure to let botanicals dry naturally if they are damp. A flower press is ideal for pressing and drying, though you may substitute a large phone book or a stack of heavy books. After they are thoroughly dried in the flower press, they may be preserved by coating them with acrylic matte varnish and allowing them to dry again. After you've affixed the botanicals to your collage, make sure to keep the piece out of the sun or strong light, as the delicate flowers or leaves can fade.

1. Collect flowers, leaves, and other botanicals. If they are damp, set them aside to dry.

2. Use a flower press (or phone book or stack of heavy books) with two pieces of matte board and white construction paper (cut to fit); use clean pieces of the white paper for each pressing.

3. Place a piece of matte board on the bottom of the press and a piece of white construction paper on top of the matte board. Place the botanical on the paper. Top with the second piece of paper, then the second piece of matte board.

4. Close the press, or top the matte board with a stack of heavy books; leave for 24 hours. Check to see if the botanical is dry; if not, change the papers if they are wet and press again until the botanical is thoroughly dry.

5. Using an old watercolor brush, coat the dried, pressed botanical with acrylic matte varnish. Keep in a dark place if not using right away; don't expose to sunlight.

Garden Poetry Journal

Collect your favorite garden quotes and poems for a beautifully illustrated journal to give or to keep. This one uses a blank photo album with heavy cream-colored pages; the protective glassine pages were removed. The marbled, leather-bound cover was pasted with a bird collage and rose scrap art, coated with gel matte medium, then wrapped with a wide ribbon and a vintage buckle. The pages were scumbled along the edges to give them a softer look, then collaged with bird ephemera, vintage wallpaper, floral scrap art, old perfume labels, and individual bird and flower collages. Poetry excerpts and quotes were written in with Olive Green ink.

"Gardening is the art that uses flowers and plants as paint, and the soil and sky as canvas."

ELIZABETH MURRAY

The Nosegay

"See how many you can identify," the donor may insist. "Revel in the color and texture, fragrance and sentiment of this nosegay," another seems to say. For no floral arrangements today ever warm the cockles of the heart as do quaint little posies in perky paper lace frills. One never wearies of creating them; no two are ever alike. They belong to the Rarissimi of Life.'

LOUISE SEYMOUR JONES
1934

COLLAGE TECHNIQUE

The left side of the journal's title-page spread was pasted with a
color copy of a collage created from a scumbled antique French
document, bird scrap art, floral wallpaper, and a scumbled antique
French banknote. The right-hand page was collaged with a flower
cut from the same wallpaper and an antique perfume label; the
journal title was written using Olive Green ink.

MATERIALS

Photo album with cream-colored pages, antique French document, Arches hot-press watercolor block, antique wallpaper, bird cut from print, antique French banknote, perfume label, watercolors, gouache, scumble brush, Yes! paste, paste brush, heavy book, Brilliant Gold gouache, filbert brush, X-acto knife, pointed scissors, Dr. Ph. Martin's Olive Green transparent watercolor ink, calligraphy pen, Titanium Buff acrylic paint, fixative, color-copy machine

A Rose is
a rose .....

'When I place a flower
on my night table
and sketch it faithfully,
it seems to me,
little by little,
I comprehend the
secret of creation.'

SHIKI

'And I will make Thee beds of roses

And a Thousand fragrant posies,

A cup of flowers, and a Kirtle

Embroidered all with leaves of myrtle.'

CHRISTOPHER MARLOWE (1564–1593)
extract from 'The Passionate Shepard to His Love'

COLLAGE TECHNIQUE

The left-hand page was pasted with a color copy of a bird collage
made with decorative paper, scrap art, and vintage postcards.
(See the process on pages 86–87 for making bird collages.) The
right-hand page was pasted with vintage scrap art roses. The
antique perfume label was pasted on to overlap the roses.
The quotes were written in with Olive Green watercolor ink.

MATERIALS

Bird collage, vintage scrap art, antique perfume label, Yes! paste,
paste brush, paper-covered brick, Dr. Ph. Martin's Olive Green
transparent watercolor ink, calligraphy pen

MATERIALS

Arches hot-press watercolor block, decorative paper, vintage postcard, scrap art rose, antique French document, cutout bird from antique book print, French stamp, rubber stamp with Paris cancellation mark, ink pad, X-acto knife, watercolor board for mounting, Yes! paste, paste brush, paper-covered brick, heavy book, scissors

PROCESS

1. On the Arches hot-press watercolor block, paste down a square piece of the antique French document. Paste decorative rice paper over the document, leaving a slight border free. Weight with the heavy book and let dry.

2. Paste the image of steps with roses, cut from a vintage postcard, on the bottom of the document; weight with the paper-covered brick and let dry.

3. Paste the vintage scrap art rose on the upper left corner. Weight with the paper-covered brick and let dry.

4. Using an X-acto knife, cut out around the top of the central petal of the postcard rose. Paste the bird image, cut from an antique German book, on the page, carefully fitting the branch that the bird is perched on into the cut around the rose petal. Weight with the paper-covered brick and let dry.

5. Paste on the French stamp and rubber-stamp with the postage cancellation mark.

Bird Notes & Quotes Journal

A journal for bird-watchers, this little book combines old sheet music, bird images, and notes and quotes about birds. A small blank journal was covered with antique sheet music and cloth binding tape on the spine. Buttons and a satin ribbon attached to a wooden feather ornament were used as a closure device. Scraps of the sheet music were also used throughout the journal for page decoration carrying the theme of birdsong throughout.

MATERIALS

Blank journal, antique music score, self-adhesive binding cloth tape, copies of collages, buttons, waxed linen thread, wood carved feather, ribbon, bone folder, X-acto knife, ruler, Yes! paste, paste brush, Japanese screw punch, awl, paper-covered brick, Walnut Stain ink, calligraphy pen, .005 Micron black pen, circle template, bird stamps

MATERIALS

Vintage postcards, wallpaper, antique ephemera (including letters, music scores, and stamps), scrap art, Arm & Hammer vintage card set of birds, decorative papers, watercolors and brushes, gouache, scumbling brush, Brilliant Gold gouache, Yes! paste, paste brush, paper-covered brick, filbert brush for Brilliant Gold gouache, color copier

PROCESS

1. Make bird collages by pasting torn old sheet music on pieces of vintage postcards that have been cut into squares. Parts of the postcards are left exposed, and some of the details on the cards show through the pasted-on music. Scumble the surface with watercolors and Permanent White gouache. (*See page 41 for scumbling technique.*)

2. Paste the cards with fragments and leaves or flowers cut from antique wallpaper and scrap art of flowers, insects, and birds, along with birds cut from advertising cards. Add postage stamps.

3. Edge the cards with Brilliant Gold gouache and spray with fixative. Copy the cards on a color copier (so they can be used again) and paste the copies on the left-hand journal pages.

4. On the right-hand journal pages, write quotes and lines of poetry about birds in Walnut Stain ink using the calligraphy pen.

5. Paste a strip of music score on the right side of each right-hand page. Paste a bird postage stamp overlapping the bottom of each strip of music. Draw in a cancellation circle using a .005 Micron black pen and a circle template.

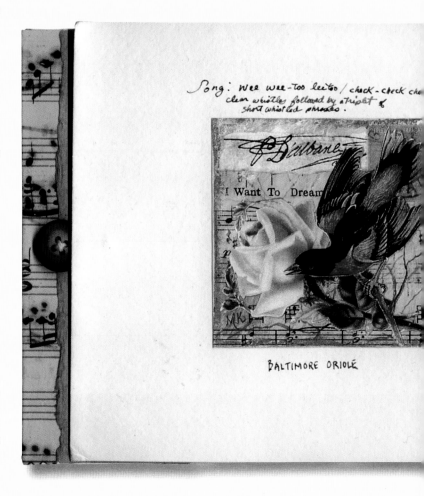

Sweet is the breath of morn,
her rising sweet,
With charm of earliest birds.

JOHN MILTON
Paradise Lost

How falls it, Oriole, thou hast come to fly
In tropic splendor through our northern sky?

At some glad moment was it Nature's choice
To dower a scrap of sunset with a voice?

Or did an orange tulip, flaked with black,
In some forgotten garden, ages back,

Yearning toward Heaven until
its wish was heard,
Desire unspeakably to be a bird?

EDGAR FAWCETT

Garden Record Journal 👉

This month-by-month weekly garden journal was created using an old-fashioned accountant's ledger. A garden record journal can become a valued keepsake and at the same time help you plan your garden for the coming year. This ledger was found in an antique shop, and its cover was collaged with a piece of vintage wallpaper border, topped with an antique French decorative monogrammed plate. Dresden leaves were pasted on two corners, then brushed with Walnut Stain ink for a vintage look. Botanical prints were used to collage the interior of the journal.

January

February

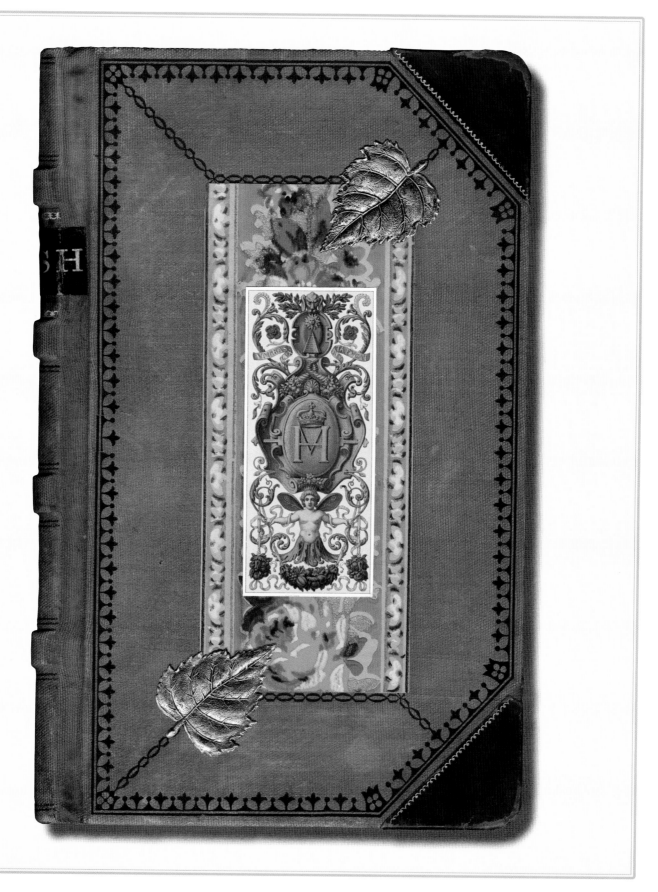

COLLAGE TECHNIQUE

The inside covers of the ledger were already covered in a wonderful marbled paper. A nameplate was added to the inside front cover using a vintage calling card.

A botanical print was pasted on an antique French document, then pasted on the first page. Light green self-adhesive binding tape was added to the spine to cover some partial damage to the inside of the ledger.

MATERIALS

Vintage ledger, botanical print, antique French document-cover paper, vintage calling card, self-adhesive binding cloth tape, ruler, X-acto knife, Yes! paste, paste brush, Sennelier Walnut Stain ink, calligraphy pen, heavy book, paper-covered brick

PROCESS

1. Paste a botanical print to an antique French document or piece of wallpaper, then paste the mounted image on the right-hand page of the journal. Weight with the paper-covered brick and let dry.

2. Brush Brilliant Gold gouache on the edges of the back of the vintage calling card; let dry. Paste the card on the left-hand page to serve as a nameplate. Write in the name of the journal-keeper using Walnut Stain ink.

3. Cover the original journal binding with self-adhesive binding cloth tape in a solid color.

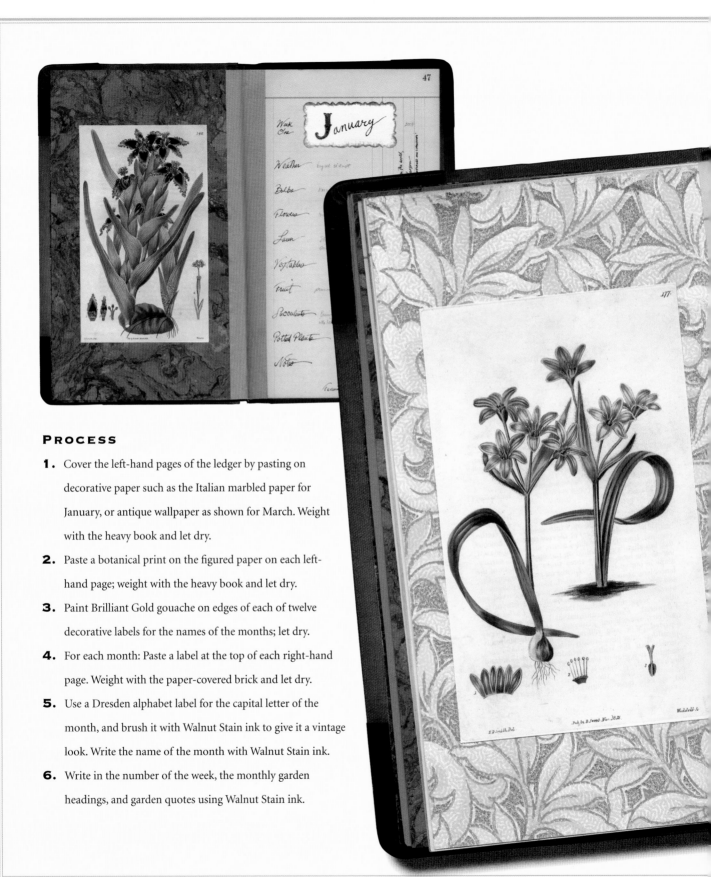

Process

1. Cover the left-hand pages of the ledger by pasting on decorative paper such as the Italian marbled paper for January, or antique wallpaper as shown for March. Weight with the heavy book and let dry.

2. Paste a botanical print on the figured paper on each left-hand page; weight with the heavy book and let dry.

3. Paint Brilliant Gold gouache on edges of each of twelve decorative labels for the names of the months; let dry.

4. For each month: Paste a label at the top of each right-hand page. Weight with the paper-covered brick and let dry.

5. Use a Dresden alphabet label for the capital letter of the month, and brush it with Walnut Stain ink to give it a vintage look. Write the name of the month with Walnut Stain ink.

6. Write in the number of the week, the monthly garden headings, and garden quotes using Walnut Stain ink.

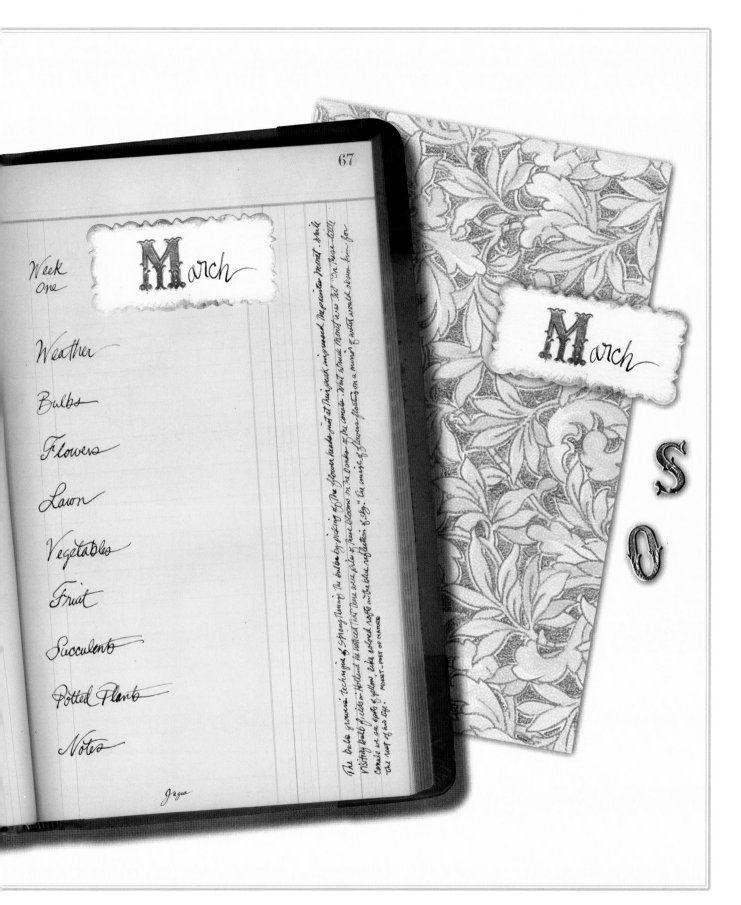

Week
One

March

Weather

Bulbs

Flowers

Lawn

Vegetables

Fruit

Succulents

Potted Plants

Notes

The bulbs growing technique of Spring timing. The bulbs by picking 750 The flowers heads must at this peak in ground. The plantin moist. While visiting beds of vides or Holland the noticed that there were piles of peat become on the border of the canals. What struck Monet was that "In those little canals we see eyes of yellow, like colored reefts in the blue reflection of sky." An image of flowers floating on a mirror of water would skinn him for the most of his life.

MONET — POET OF NATURE

March

S

O

My Parents loved the ocean and Trees.....

OBITAS BEACH 8/5/31

{ Family Keepsake Journals }

Family Vacation Journal 101

Grandmother's Journal 109

Family Keepsake Journals, from baby books to anniversary and birthday celebrations to records of holiday trips, naturally lend themselves to being collaged with photographs and mementos. The two journals here, one a re-created family vacation from the past, the other a grandmother's loving record of the birth and early years of her two grand-daughters, show how imagination and the art of collage can create priceless family keepsakes.

Family Vacation Journal

An Italian watercolor journal covered with marbled paper became the journal that the artist's parents might have made of their road trips to the California coast in the 1930s. A picture of an old car traveling through the redwoods, taken from a vintage menu cover, was pasted on the cover, and a ribbon with a vintage buckle was fastened around the book. The interior combines maps, postcards, and real photographs of the young couple to create a touching tribute to them and to the past.

COLLAGE TECHNIQUE

To create an ocean beach atmosphere for these two
pages, decorative Japanese paper with a wave motif
was pasted on each page. Copies of two painted
ocean scenes, torn on the edges to
soften them, were pasted on the
Japanese paper. Photocopies of
photographs of the artist's parents
were mounted with vintage photo
corners to overlap the ocean paintings.
Text was written on the paintings and
photocopies using Walnut Stain ink.

it's what drew them to Big Sur.

COLLAGE TECHNIQUE

Ephemera collected from antique-paper shows and other sources
was used to create the forested atmosphere of the Big Sur region.
Above journal pages: An advertising photo of an old car in the
redwoods, taken from a 1922 Standard Oil magazine, was pasted on
the left-hand page. An old map from an advertisement for Monterey
County was pasted on the right-hand page. A piece of torn marbled
paper the color of redwood bark was pasted on, overlapping the map.
Two photocopies of photos in sepia tones were mounted on the
paper; they show the mother and father next to their car before
beginning the trip down the coast from San Francisco.

Left journal pages: Paper made from bark pulp was pasted on both pages. On the left-hand page, a picture of a deer from the 1922 magazine was edged with Brilliant Gold gouache, then pasted on the paper. A decorative card label was pasted above it, and a quote about trees was written on it in Walnut Stain ink. A strip of Japanese wave paper was pasted down the center of the bark paper on the right-hand page. Photocopies of photos were mounted on the wave paper using vintage black photo corners. Scrap art of botanicals was pasted on to overlap one photo.

MATERIALS

Bark paper (handmade from bark pulp), decorative Japanese wave paper, vintage 1922 Standard Oil magazine, vintage advertising map, scrap art botanicals, photocopies of old photos in sepia tones, vintage black photo corners, decorative label, Yes! paste, paste brush, Brilliant Gold gouache, filbert brush for gouache, heavy book, paper-covered brick

MATERIALS

Decorative paper with fern imprint, decorative Japanese paper with wave motif, sepia photocopies of old photographs, vintage black photo mounts, scrap art botanicals, cutout illustrations of trout and fly fishing pouch photocopied from Maryjo Koch's book (*Pond Lake River Sea*), Yes! paste, ribbon, paste brush, Japanese screw punch, heavy book, paper-covered brick, Walnut Stain ink, calligraphy pen

PROCESS

1. Far left journal page: Paste on decorative paper with fern imprint, leaving a small border of page bare; weight with a heavy book and let dry. Mount photocopies of photos on the page using vintage photo mounts. Paste the scrap art of botanicals to overlap one of the photos; weight with the paper-covered brick and let dry.

2. Above journal pages: Paste the Japanese wave paper on both pages; weight with the heavy book to dry. Mount sepia photocopies of old photos on both pages using vintage photo mounts. Paste a cutout copy of an illustration, here a trout from the artist's book *Pond Lake River Sea,* overlapping a photo; weight with the paper-covered brick and let dry.

3. Paste a cutout illustration of a fly-fishing pouch on heavy paper; weight with the paper-covered brick and let dry. Punch a hole through the top of the mounted pouch and through the journal page with a Japanese screw punch. Thread the ribbon through the hole in the page and tie it on the pouch. Paste a vintage shipping tag on front of the pouch and write the text using Walnut Stain ink.

COLLAGE TECHNIQUE

Inside cover (left-hand page): The cutout border of a scrap art card
was pasted inside the cover to use as a nameplate. The name and
address were written in using Olive Green ink. A lace ribbon was tied
around the front cover, threaded through the vintage buckle on the
front, and tied closed. Self-adhesive cloth binding tape was affixed
to the gutter of the book to unify the two opening pages.

On the right-hand page, a vintage bookmark of a child's face in
a daffodil was pasted on. More vintage scrap art of a rose with a
child's face was pasted on to overlap the bookmark. A self-adhesive
bee sticker was added, and the title written in with Olive Green ink.

Grandmother's Journal

A small blank journal with deckled pages becomes a grandmother's memory book when illustrated with vintage scrap art of flowers and babies and real photographs of grandchildren. It was created to commemorate the birth of the artist's grandchildren. The cover (below) was pasted with vintage wallpaper and bound with colored cloth binding tape sealed on the edge with a floral trim. Two vintage scrap art nests with babies hatching from eggs represent the two granddaughters, one with light hair, the other with dark. A lace ribbon fastened with a small vintage belt buckle completes the cover.

We joyfully announce
the birth of our daughter

Olivia Grace

February 2, 2003

8 pounds 2.8 ounces

21 inches

Wendy and Ken Candelaria

COLLAGE TECHNIQUE

Above journal pages: The birth announcement was pasted on the left-hand page. A scrap art rose was pasted on to overlap the announcement. Notes about the granddaughter's birth were written on the right-hand page in Olive Green ink. A vintage scrap art rose and vintage label of a rabbit were pasted below the text.

Journal pages, below: A baby photo was mounted on the left-hand page with cream-colored photo tabs; a vintage scrap art rose was pasted on the right-hand page. Vintage scrap art clowns were pasted over the rose, and text was written in with Olive Green ink.

On February 2, 2003, I became a grandmother and then again on May 12, 2004. Both my grandchildren have brought such joy into my life.

The fragrance of a baby is a rose to the nose!

MATERIALS

Small blank journal with deckled edges, photos, birth announcement, vintage scrap art roses, vintage rabbit label, vintage scrap art clowns, cream photo mounts, Yes! paste, paste brush, Dr. Ph. Martin's Olive Green ink, calligraphy pen, paper-covered brick

Olivia is 19 weeks old!

June 9th 2003

COLLAGE TECHNIQUE

Above journal pages: The left-hand page was pasted with a tea party invitation tag (made from folded card stock with a transferred image on the cover; *see page 114 for image transfer technique*) and a scrap art bee. The right-hand page combines a small photo of a grandchild with a vintage advertising card photograph, a cutout photo of the child, and a vintage scrap art hand label.

Lower left journal pages: A vintage advertising card of a child riding a bird was mounted on the left-hand page; the right-hand page was collaged with the cutout decorative border of a vintage card, a cutout photo, and a vintage scrap art rose; the rose stem was painted in with watercolor.

MATERIALS

Card stock, transfer image of a girl with teacup, Chartpak blender pen (P-O 201), watercolors, ribbon, decorative leaf, Japanese screw punch, vintage scrap art rose, bee, hand label, vintage advertising cards (girl on bird, teapot, and teacup), vintage card border, photos, cream photo mount corners, small pointed scissors, X-acto knife, 45-degree triangle, watercolors, watercolor brush, Yes! paste, paste brush, paper-covered brick

COLLAGE TECHNIQUE: IMAGE TRANSFERS

Image transfers are one of the easiest ways to add artwork to a journal; any image that can be photocopied can be transferred onto a smooth, unshiny surface. Your own photographs and original art will add to the unique look of your journal, while antique clip art will enrich your collage work and give your journal a vintage look.

PROCESS

1. Photocopy an image in black and white using a copy machine with a toner cartridge. Using white paper tape, tape the copy face down on the surface you're transferring it to.

2. Using a new blender pen, rub over the back of a section of the copy, completely and evenly covering the section.

3. With an older, partially dried-out blender pen, repeat the process over the same section, using more pressure. Repeat Steps 2 and 3 until the whole image is covered.

4. Lift a corner of the copy to make sure the image was thoroughly transferred. If not, repeat Step 2. Discard the copy when finished.

{ Clip Art }

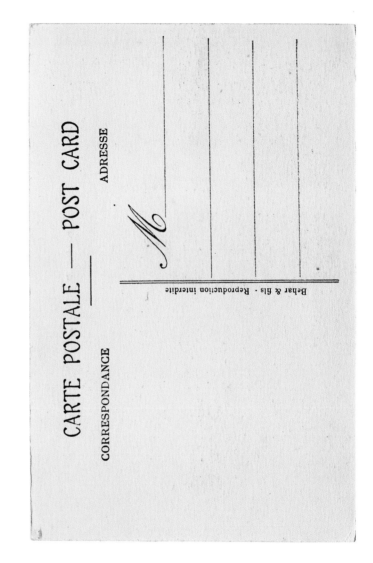

{ Clip Art }

MENU

Potage Crème d'Argenteuil

Barbue à l'Amiral

Filet Rossini

Salmis de Faisans grand Veneur

Marquises Moët et Chandon

Poulardes de Bresse truffées

Chaud-froid de Mauviettes

à la Maréchale

Salade

Croûte de Champignons

Glace Montreuil

Dessert.

MENU
du 19 Mars 1906

Consommé Tosca

Langouste à la Moderne

Timbale Mirabeau

Poulardes braisées à la Richelieu

Jambons de Prague truffés à la Orloff

Salade

Petits Pois nouveaux à l'Anglaise

Galantine de Caneton Rossini

Glace Églantine

Dessert

{ *Clip Art* }

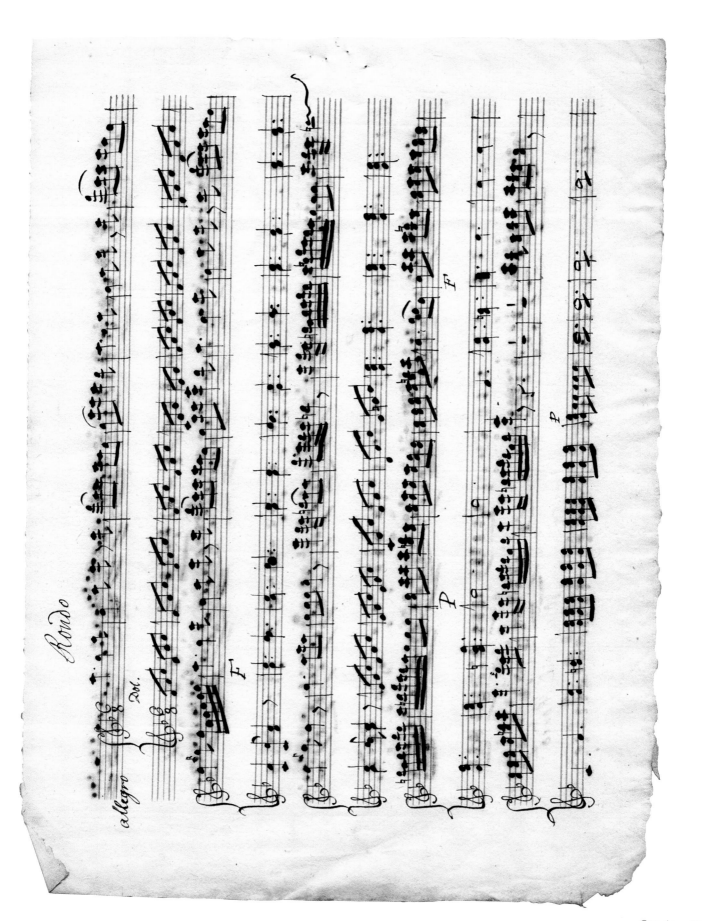

{ *Resources* }

Most of the materials and tools listed below are available in art and craft stores, but they can often also be ordered directly from the manufacturer. Look for vintage materials such as stamps, postcards, letters, and wallpaper trim at flea markets, antique stores, paper fairs, and secondhand shops and on the Internet; new and reproduced materials are available in craft stores and on the Internet.

Aria
1522 Grant Avenue
San Francisco, CA 94133
415-433-0219
Antique French documents, letters, music scores, antique French ephemera.

Cavallini & Company
401 Forbes Boulevard
South San Francisco, CA 94080
800-226-5287
www.cavallini.com
Decorative papers, cards, maps, posters.

Findings, a Sewing Emporium
Nancy King-Monk
San Carlos between Ocean and Seventh
Carmel, California 93921
P.O. Box 6638
831-624-3700
Ribbons, vintage ribbons, lace, fabric, thread, linen thread, sewing supplies, vintage buttons, vintage buckles, vintage sewing supplies.

Koch Studios: Maryjo Koch
www.kochstudios.com
Original artwork, books, cards, classes, step-by-step art lessons.

Lenz Arts
142 River Street
Santa Cruz, CA 95060
831-423-1935
www.lenzarts.com
Decorative papers, art supplies, brushes.

Palace Art
1501 41st Avenue
Capitola, CA 95010
831-464-2700/800-275-8777
www.gopalaceart.com
Decorative papers, art supplies, Simply Simmons scumbling brushes, paints.

Paper Artique
Lisa Ford
www.paperartique.com
Antique wallpaper.

Paper Source
Stores nationwide
888-PAPER-11
www.paper-source.com
Yes! paste, paste brushes, awls, bone folders, rubber stamps, ink pads, decorative papers, ribbon, bookmaking supplies, KHADI blank journals, decorative journals, glassine envelopes, wax seals.

Bruce Shyer
986 Grosvenor Place
Oakland, CA 94610
510-763-8828
Antique and vintage paper ephemera.

Daniel Smith
4150 First Avenue South
Seattle, WA 98124
800-426-6740
www.danielsmith.com
Watercolors, gouache, oxgall liquid, Sennelier walnut stain ink, Pigma Micron ink pens, matte medium, Indian Village handmade watercolor paper, decorative papers, awls, Japanese screw punches, Yes! paste, brushes.

Sherry Sonnett
2040 Rodney Drive, No. 26
Los Angeles, CA 90027
323-662-4600
paperdoggy@yahoo.com
Antique and vintage paper ephemera.

Susan's Store Room
Susan Hoy
239 San Anselmo Avenue
San Anselmo, CA 94960
415-456-1333
www.susansstoreroom.com
Dresden ornaments, antique scrap art, art supplies, cards, antiques, rubber stamp.

Vintage Paper Fair
415-668-1636
www.vintagepaperfair.com
An annual paper fair held in cities across the United States.

{ Notes }

{ *Notes* }

{ *Acknowledgments* }

I gratefully thank my book packager Jennifer Barry, for her exquisite concept and design—a lovely collaboration; Kristen Hall, for her technical and creative assistance; my writer, Carolyn Miller, for her help in putting my techniques into words and her close attention to detail; Wendy Candelaria, for her keen photographic eye and loving support, and Ken, Olivia, and Catherine, for sharing Hawaii with me; Sunny Koch and Jonathan Koch, for their creative support and encouragement; Lisa Ford, for her fantastic collection of antique wallpaper, which she so generously shares; Laura Belt, for her dear friendship and the fabulous treasures and embellishments that she is constantly searching out and sharing with me; Rockport Publishers, for making this book a reality; and my students, family, and friends, for enriching my artistic journey.

{ *Index* }

Motorbooks International

POWERPRO SERIES

FUEL INJECTION
Installation, Performance Tuning, Modifications

Jeff Hartman

First published in 1993 by Motorbooks International Publishers & Wholesalers, PO Box 2, 729 Prospect Avenue, Osceola, WI 54020 USA

Motorbooks International books are also available at discounts in bulk quantity for industrial or sales-promotional use. For details write to Special Sales Manager at the Publisher's address

Selected illustrations are used courtesy of Jan P. Norbye from his book, Automotive Fuel Injection Systems: A Technical Guide (Motorbooks International).

Library of Congress Cataloging-in-Publication Data
Hartman, Jeff.
    Fuel injection: installation, performance tuning, modification/Jeff Hartman.
        p. cm. – – (Motorbooks International powerpro series)
    Includes bibliographical references and index.
    ISBN 0-87938-743-2
    1. Automobiles– –Motors– –Electronic fuel injection systems.
I. Title. II. Series.
TL214.F78H37   1993
629.25'3– –dc20   93-13168

On the front cover: A Chevrolet small-block V-8 uses a complete Edelbrock Pro-Flo fuel injection system. The system has an Edelbrock control unit that provides users with diagnostic data on an LCD unit, eliminating the need to use a personal computer for tuning. *Edelbrock*

Printed and bound in the United States of America